YOU WILL BE A GREAT ACTOR

You Will Be a Great Actor

Read Daily for Affirmation Book Series

Walter the Educator

Silent King Books

SILENT KING BOOKS

SKB

Copyright © 2024 by Walter the Educator

All rights reserved. No part of this book may be reproduced in any manner whatsoever without written permission except in the case of brief quotations embodied in critical articles and reviews.

First Printing, 2024

Disclaimer
This book is a literary work; poems are not about specific persons, locations, situations, and/or circumstances unless mentioned in a historical context. This book is for entertainment and informational purposes only. The author and publisher offer this information without warranties expressed or implied. No matter the grounds, neither the author nor the publisher will be accountable for any losses, injuries, or other damages caused by the reader's use of this book. The use of this book acknowledges an understanding and acceptance of this disclaimer.

I pray that you will be a great actor.

For where two or three are gathered together in my name, there am I in the midst of them - Matthew 18:20

YOU WILL BE A GREAT ACTOR

Improvisation, the art of the now,

You Will Be A GREAT ACTOR

In spontaneity, I've taken a vow.

You Will Be A
GREAT
ACTOR

To live in the moment, raw and real,

You Will Be A GREAT ACTOR

In the flux of creation, I find my zeal.

You Will Be A GREAT ACTOR

Costumes and makeup, the tools of disguise,

You Will Be A
GREAT
ACTOR

Transforming me in the audience's eyes.

You Will Be A GREAT ACTOR

Yet beneath the layers, my essence remains,

You Will Be A GREAT ACTOR

A vessel of stories, tethered by invisible chains.

You Will Be A GREAT ACTOR

Lights dim, the hush before the storm,

You Will Be A
GREAT
ACTOR

In that silence, I find my norm.

You Will Be A
GREAT
ACTOR

The roar of applause, a symphony sweet,

You Will Be A GREAT ACTOR

Echoes of triumph, in each heartbeat.

You Will Be A GREAT ACTOR

"I will be a great actor," I declare with pride,

You Will Be A GREAT ACTOR

In the theatre of life, where dreams collide.

You Will Be A GREAT ACTOR

Through laughter and sorrow, my path is clear,

You Will Be A
GREAT
ACTOR

To evoke emotions, to draw others near.

You Will Be A GREAT ACTOR

Each character I play, a mirror to the soul,

You Will Be A GREAT ACTOR

Reflecting the human condition, making me whole.

You Will Be A GREAT ACTOR

In their stories, I find my voice,

You Will Be A GREAT ACTOR

In their struggles, I rejoice.

You Will Be A
GREAT
ACTOR

For acting is not just a craft or a skill,

You Will Be A GREAT ACTOR

It's a calling, a fire, an unquenchable thrill.

You Will Be A
GREAT
ACTOR

To step into another's shoes, to see through their eyes,

You Will Be A
GREAT
ACTOR

To breathe life into words, to soar to the skies.

You Will Be A GREAT ACTOR

So I stand tall, in the spotlight's glare,

You Will Be A
GREAT
ACTOR

With a heart full of dreams, I lay my soul bare.

You Will Be A GREAT ACTOR

"I will be a great actor," I proclaim with might,

You Will Be A GREAT ACTOR

In the tapestry of performance, my spirit takes flight.

You Will Be A GREAT ACTOR

The road ahead is winding and steep,

You Will Be A
GREAT
ACTOR

But with each challenge, I delve deep.

You Will Be A
GREAT
ACTOR

For in every role, a piece of me resides,

You Will Be A GREAT ACTOR

In the theatre of dreams, where destiny abides.

You Will Be A
GREAT
ACTOR

As the final curtain falls, and the stage is bare,

You Will Be A GREAT ACTOR

I reflect on my journey, the moments we share.

You Will Be A GREAT ACTOR

For in this art, I find my truth,

You Will Be A
GREAT
ACTOR

In the boundaries potential of eternal youth.

You Will Be A GREAT ACTOR

"I will be a great actor," this promise I keep,

You Will Be A GREAT ACTOR

In the theatre of life, where memories seep.

You Will Be A
GREAT
ACTOR

With passion, persistence, and unwavering heart,

You Will Be A GREAT ACTOR

I embrace my destiny, ready to depart.

You Will Be A
GREAT
ACTOR

ABOUT THE CREATOR

Walter the Educator is one of the pseudonyms for Walter Anderson. Formally educated in Chemistry, Business, and Education, he is an educator, an author, a diverse entrepreneur, and he is the son of a disabled war veteran. "Walter the Educator" shares his time between educating and creating. He holds interests and owns several creative projects that entertain, enlighten, enhance, and educate, hoping to inspire and motivate you.

Follow, find new works, and stay up to date
with Walter the Educator™
at WaltertheEducator.com